Jennifer Space Car

Richard Edwards

OXFORD
UNIVERSITY PRESS

OXFORD
UNIVERSITY PRESS

Great Clarendon Street, Oxford OX2 6DP

Oxford University Press is a department of the University of Oxford.
It furthers the University's objective of excellence in research, scholarship,
and education by publishing worldwide in

Oxford New York
Athens Auckland Bangkok Bogotá Buenos Aires Calcutta
Cape Town Chennai Dar es Salaam Delhi Florence Hong Kong Istanbul
Karachi Kuala Lumpur Madrid Melbourne Mexico City Mumbai
Nairobi Paris São Paulo Singapore Taipei Tokyo Toronto Warsaw

and associated companies in Berlin Ibadan

Oxford is a trade mark of Oxford University Press
in the UK and in certain other countries

Text © Richard Edwards 2000
First published 2000

All rights reserved. No part of this publication may be reproduced,
stored in a retrieval system, or transmitted, in any form or by any means,
without the prior permission in writing of Oxford University Press,
or as expressly permitted by law, or under terms agreed with the appropriate
reprographics rights organisation. Enquiries concerning reproduction
outside the scope of the above should be sent to the Rights Department,
Oxford University Press, at the address above

You must not circulate this book in any other binding or cover and you must
impose this same condition on any acquiror

British Library Cataloguing in publication Data
Data available

ISBN 0 19 917328 1

Available in Packs

Stage 4–6 Pack (one of each book)   ISBN 0 19 917329 X
Stage 4–6 Class Pack (six of each book)   ISBN 0 19 917330 3

Printed in Hong Kong

Young Jennifer Jones, the inventor,
said "I think I'll invent a space car,
a car that will dart through the distant dark
and arrive at the brightest star."

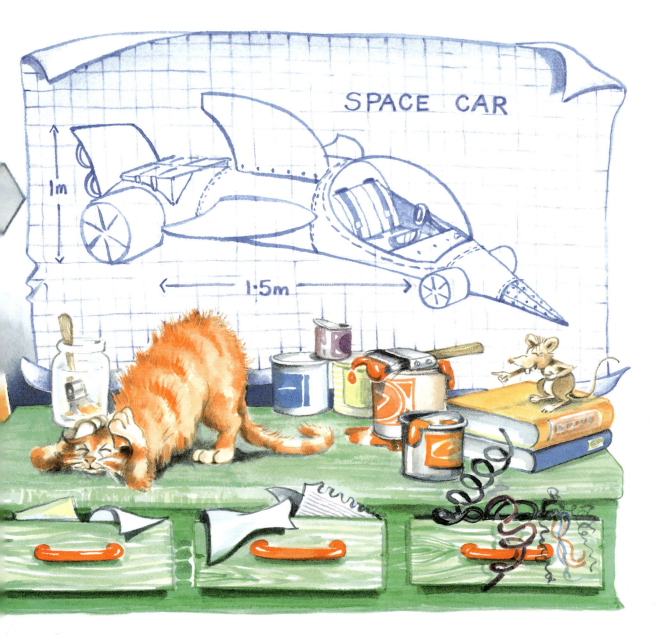

Young Jennifer Jones started working with metal and plastic and wood, building her car that would fly to a star, and hammering as hard as she could.

She cut and she glued and she nailed.
She painted it silver and black.
Her car looked so good with its bright shiny hood
and the rack which she fixed to the back.

Young Jennifer Jones climbed aboard
and checked that the tank was full.
On the rack at the back sat her dog and her cat,
as she gave the car-starter a pull.

Up into space whooshed the space car,
as young Jennifer followed her chart,
and the car lit the dark with glittering sparks
all fiery and shiny and smart.

Upwards and upwards and upwards,
past the moon and then out towards Mars,
and her dog went "Bark!" as they
flew through the dark,
and headed on out to the stars.

But when Jennifer Jones, the inventor,
arrived at the brightest star,
she caught sight of a star that was
brighter by far.
So she set out again in her car.

And onwards and onwards she travels,
so distant, so brave, and so far.
Will she ever come back with her dog and her cat,
young Jennifer in her space car?